★GETTING TO KNOW★
ITALY
and ITALIAN

Written by
Emma Sansone

Illustrated by
Kim Woolley

BARRON'S

Contents

First edition for the United States
published 1993 by Barron's Educational Series, Inc.

© copyright 1992 Times Four Publishing Ltd

First published in Great Britain in 1992 by
The Watts Group

All inquiries should be addressed to:
Barron's Educational Series, Inc.
250 Wireless Boulevard
Hauppauge, New York 11788

Library of Congress Catalog Card No.
92-38649

International Standard Book No.
0-8120-6338-4 (hardcover)
0-8120-1534-7 (paperback)

PRINTED IN BELGIUM

3456   9907   987654321

About this book

In this book you can find out about Italy — its people, landscapes, and language. For example, discover what the Italians like to eat and drink, what they do for a living, and what famous Italian places look like.

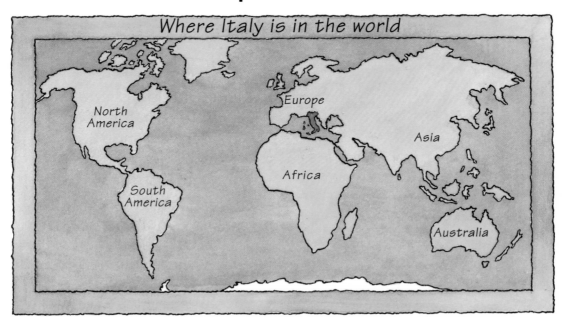

Where Italy is in the world

North America

South America

Europe

Africa

Asia

Australia

Find out, also, what school days are like for Italian children, and about their vacations and festivals. On page 26, there is a special section to introduce you to speaking Italian.

Hello!

Ciao!

It explains how to use and pronounce everyday words and phrases, so you can make friends and ask for things in cafés and shops. Also, some Italian words and their meanings are given throughout the book to help you increase your vocabulary.

Map of Italy

Italy is in southern Europe. In the north it has borders with France, Switzerland, Austria, and Slovenia. The Mediterranean Sea borders Italy to the east, west, and south. The country is easy to recognize on a map, because it is shaped like a high-heeled boot. The island of Sicily is just by the toe of Italy. The island of Sardinia is further out to the northwest.

 Highest mountain:
Mont Blanc **(Monte Bianco)**, in the Alps, 15,771 feet (4,807 meters). It is the highest mountain in western Europe and lies along the Italian-French border.

The Italian landscape is very varied. In the north, there are high mountains and a large flat plain. Along the east coast there are long beaches. The west coast is more rocky. Mountains and hills run all the way down the middle of the country, like a backbone. Some of these mountains are volcanoes.

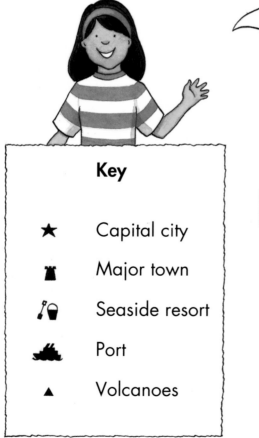

Key

★   Capital city

    Major town

    Seaside resort

    Port

▲   Volcanoes

Longest river:
River Po, 405 miles (652 km). The river flows from the Alps to the Adriatic Sea. Rice is grown in huge fields along the river valley.

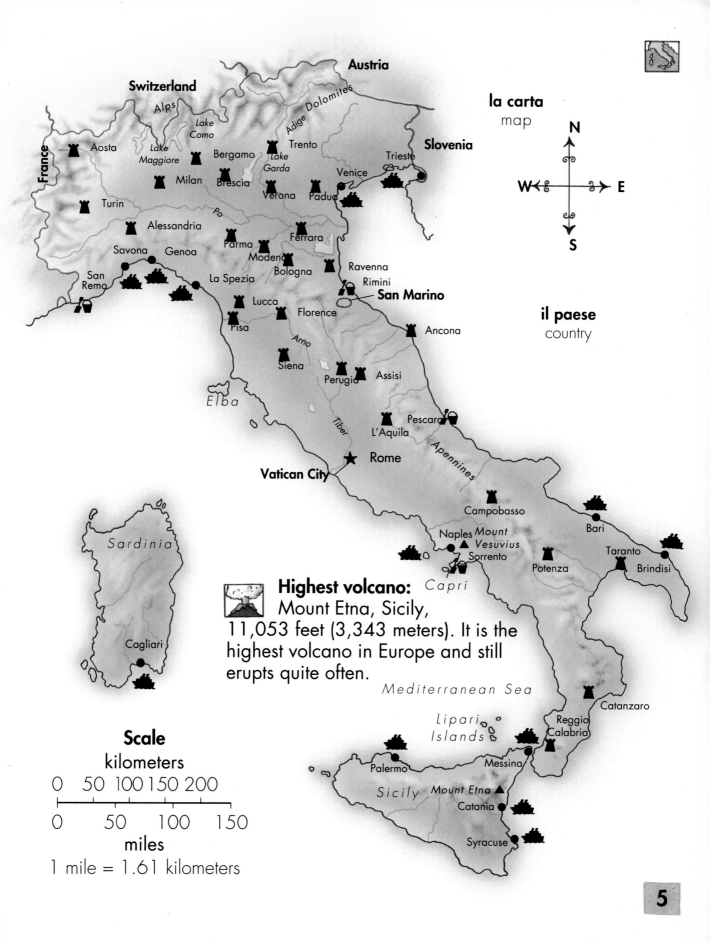

Switzerland

Austria

Alps

Dolomites

Adige

Trento

Slovenia

Trieste

Aosta

Lake Como

Lake Maggiore

Bergamo

Lake Garda

France

Milan

Brescia

Venice

Turin

Verona

Padua

Po

Alessandria

Parma

Ferrara

Savona

Genoa

Modena

Ravenna

San Remo

La Spezia

Bologna

Rimini

San Marino

Lucca

Florence

Pisa

Ancona

Arno

Elba

Siena

Perugia

Assisi

Tiber

Pescara

L'Aquila

Apennines

Rome

Vatican City

Campobasso

Bari

Naples

Mount Vesuvius

Sorrento

Taranto

Sardinia

Potenza

Brindisi

Capri

Mediterranean Sea

Cagliari

Catanzaro

Lipari Islands

Reggio Calabria

Palermo

Messina

Sicily

Mount Etna ▲

Catania

Syracuse

la carta
map

N

W — E

S

il paese
country

Highest volcano:
Mount Etna, Sicily,
11,053 feet (3,343 meters). It is the
highest volcano in Europe and still
erupts quite often.

Scale
kilometers
0 50 100 150 200

0   50   100   150
miles
1 mile = 1.61 kilometers

Facts about Italy

Italy is about the same size as New York state, but has more than twice the population. There are so many mountains that most people live in cities and towns in the plains and on the coasts.

Size: 116,303 sq miles (301,225 sq km)

la bandiera
flag

Population: 57,590,000

The Italian flag is green, white, and red. It is called the **tricolore**, which means a flag with three colors.

The Head of State is the president, who is elected by Parliament every seven years. But most important decisions about the way the country is run are made by the prime minister and the government.

Capital city: Roma (Rome)

Official name: Italia or **Repubblica Italiana** (Italian Republic)

Language

Although the official language is Italian, other languages are also spoken in parts of the country:

German is spoken by some people in the far north of Italy.

la lingua
language

In most regions of Italy, many people also speak a local variety of their language, called a dialect.

Near the French border in the northeast, some Italians speak French.

Money

Italian money is counted in **lire**. The smallest coin is 10 lire. A packet of chewing gum costs about 100 lire.

There are many different coins and bank notes. Coins are usually made in amounts of 50, 100, 200, and 500 lire. The head of a woman is shown on the coins, representing Italy.

i soldi
money

Bank notes are issued for 1,000, 2,000, 5,000, 10,000, 50,000, and 100,000 lire. The heads of famous Italian people appear on the notes.

Some things made in Italy

la pizza
pizza

l'olio d'oliva
olive oil

il vino
wine
Chianti, Asti Spumante, Barolo, Soave

la pasta
pasta
spaghetti, macaroni, vermicelli

la macchina
cars
Ferrari, Fiat, Lancia

i vestiti
clothes
Benetton, Gucci, Armani

Regions of Italy

Italy is divided into 20 regions, including the islands of Sicily and Sardinia in the Mediterranean. The scenery, weather, and way of life vary greatly from region and region.

In the south, the winter is cool, the spring is sunny and fresh, and the summer is hot and very dry.

il tempo
weather

In the north, the winter is very cold, spring and autumn are very wet, and summer is hot and dry.

la neve
snow

In the north, the high mountains of the Alps are covered with snow most of the year. There are many ski resorts for winter vacations, and in summer, people go hiking.

There are also some large lakes among the mountains. The beautiful scenery attracts many visitors.

In the mountains, there are wildlife parks, where you can find animals such as deer, chamois, mountain goats, and lynxes.

il lago
lake

Just south of the Alps is a large plain, the Pianura Padana. It is good farmland where farmers grow wheat, corn, and rice.

The western coastline is generally rocky, with many inlets. The eastern coastline is flatter, with long, sandy beaches. There are many vacation resorts along both coasts.

Tuscany, Umbria, and Latium, in central Italy, are hilly. The country-side is beautiful, with picturesque towns and villages, and castles.

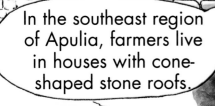

In the southeast region of Apulia, farmers live in houses with cone-shaped stone roofs.

In the south, people grow tomatoes, oranges, and lemons. Grapes are grown almost everywhere.

Southern Italy (the foot of the boot) is very rocky. Towns have been built on the steep slopes of the mountains.

Several tiny, volcanic islands lie off the west and south coasts of Italy. The rocky coastline is dotted with fishing villages.

Rome

Rome is Italy's capital city. It is also the largest city in Italy. Nearly three million people live there.

It is a very ancient city. Originally it was built on seven hills beside the River Tiber, about 15 miles (25 km) from the sea. The ancient Romans conquered most of Europe, and Rome was the capital of their empire. You can still see some of their ancient monuments, like the Colosseum and the ruins of the Roman Forum.

Now the city has grown so much that the outskirts reach almost to the sea, and traffic problems are terrible.

You can get around Rome by bus, but the fastest way is by **Metro** — the subway.

In the center, there are many beautiful churches, squares, and fountains. There are cafés all around, where people like to sit outside, drink coffee, and eat ice cream.

Colosseo
(ancient Roman arena)

Monumento a Vittoria Emanuele
(built to celebrate the unification of Italy)

Pantheon
(Roman temple to the
gods, which later became a
Christian church)

Arco di Constantino
(ancient Roman arch
built to celebrate
Emperor Constantine)

Basilica di San Pietro
(huge Roman Catholic
church in Vatican City,
home of the Pope)

**Piazza di Spagna and the
Spanish Steps**
(beautiful square with a
long staircase and a
fountain shaped like a boat)

Fontana di Trevi
(people say that if you throw
a coin into this fountain, you
are sure to return to Roman
one day)

In a typical Italian town

Most Italian towns and villages are built around a square. There is usually a church on one side, shops, and at least one café. When it is sunny, the café has tables outside.

la gelateria
ice cream shop

l'edicola/il giornalaio
newspaper stand

la chiesa
church

la tabaccheria
tabacconist

il caffé
café

FARMACIA

l'ufficio postale
post office

la farmacia
pharmacy

la macelleria
butcher shop

We generally wear navy blue uniforms in winter, white uniforms in summer, and white helmets.

i vigili urbani
town police

Old people like to sit in the square with their friends and watch what is going on. Young people often meet their friends in the café.

The church plays an important part in village life. On Sunday mornings, families dress up and go to Mass. Most people in Italy are Roman Catholics.

alimentari/la drogheria
grocery store

la libreria
bookshop

la banca
bank

l'ufficio turistico
tourist office

la cartoleria
stationery store

la pasticceria
pastry shop

il supermercato
supermarket

il negozio di abbigliamento
clothing store

il municipio
town hall

la panetteria
bakery

il negozio di ferramenta
hardware store

Eating in Italy

Italians love their food and enjoy eating out. Each region of Italy has its own special foods.

Italians don't eat much for breakfast. Children normally have a cup of milk and some biscuits or bread and jam. Adults like to put coffee in their milk. Some have a little cup of strong black coffee on its own.

People often have a snack **(uno spuntino)** half way through the morning. Children eat this in school.

la colazione
breakfast

il caffè
coffee

il pane
bread

il latte
milk

la marmellata
jam

il burro
butter

Lunch **(il pranzo)** is usually between 1 P.M. and 2 P.M. People normally start with pasta or rice. The second course is usually meat or fish, with bread and vegetables or a salad. The meal ends with fresh fruit. Desserts are only eaten on Sundays or on special occasions.

Supper **(la cena)** is in the evening, between 7 P.M. and 9 P.M. The first course can be pasta, rice, or soup. Then people normally eat cheese and cold meats, or an omelette, with bread and vegetables. They finish with fresh fruit again.

Some typical Italian dishes:

risotto alla milanese
rice cooked with stock, white wine, and saffron

pizza alla napoletana
pizza with mozzarella cheese, tomato, anchovy, and oregano

spaghetti alla bolognese
spaghetti with a meat sauce

saltimbocca alla romana
little slices of veal with ham, sage, and sweet wine

pesce spada alla griglia
grilled swordfish cutlets

peperonata
peppers cooked with onions and tomatoes

lasagne
layers of wide pasta, baked with meat sauce and cheese

gelato
ice cream

torrone
hard nougat with almonds or hazelnuts

zabaglione
warm creamy dessert made with eggs yolks, sugar, and sweet wine

vino
wine
Barolo, Chianti, Soave

aperitivo
before-dinner drink
Martini, Campari

birra
beer
Peroni

limonata
lemonade

Drinks

What people do

In Italy, people live and work differently in the various regions. There are large industrial areas where people work in factories. Some people work as farmers in the countryside. Tourism also provides many jobs.

la fabbrica
factory

Industry has grown quickly in Italy. More people now work in industry than in farming. Most of the factories are in the north, around the great cities of Milan, Turin, and Genoa.

Many people in Milan work in the fashion and textile industries.

Pottery and leather goods are made in Tuscany and Umbria. Venice is famous for its beautiful ornamental glass.

Italy also produces ships, cars, chemicals, machinery, and electrical goods such as computers.

The tourist industry employs many people, especially along the coasts, by the lakes, and in the Alps. They run hotels, restaurants, cafés, and bars.

l'uva
grapes

Wine is very important in Italy. There are vineyards in almost every region. Some grapes are grown to be eaten, but most are made into wine. Some Italian wines are very famous, and are sold all over the world.

Around the coast there are many ports, and fishing is very important. A large number of people work in the fishing industry.

il pescatore
fisherman

l'agricoltore
farmer

Cattle are kept on the plains and in some rich pastures in the Alps. Further south, in the Apennine mountains, farmers keep sheep. **Pecorino** and **Parmigiano** cheeses are made from sheep's milk.

le pecore
sheep

le mucche
cows

Olives are grown all over Italy except in the far north. They are used for making olive oil, and for eating.

l'oliva
olive

Peaches, nectarines, apricots, plums, oranges, lemons, and tomatoes are grown all along the west and east coasts. Many are exported to the rest of Europe.

17

Children in Italy

Here you can find out something about school life in Italy, and about how Italian children spend their time.

la scuola
school

The school day usually begins at 8:30 in the morning, and ends around 1 o'clock. Then children go home for lunch. There is no school in the afternoon, but there is homework to do every day. Many children also have to go to school on Saturdays.

Italian children have no midterm vacation, but their summer vacation is quite long.

i compiti
homework

We have two weeks of vacation at Christmas, two weeks at Easter, and nearly three months in the summer.

Most Italian families take their vacations in Italy. In the summer, they may go to the seaside or to the mountains to get away from the heat.

le vacanze
vacations

Because the summer vacation is so long, most children have to do **i compiti delle vacanze** (vacation homework) to review what they learned at school during the year.

i ragazzi
children

In most Italian schools, pupils do not wear a uniform. In elementary schools, children wear blue or black overalls on top of their clothes, so they won't get too dirty.

Older children like to wear jeans and sweatshirts and fashionable sneakers.

There is not much time for sports in Italian schools. Children who like sports generally practice them in the afternoons. Soccer is the most popular sport with boys. Many girls like volleyball and basketball. Swimming and tennis are popular in the summer.

Schools in the north of Italy often take their pupils on a **settimana bianca** (white week) in January or February. The whole class spends a week in a ski resort. They have some lessons, but spend most of the time skiing, tobogganing, and practicing winter sports.

Italian children enjoy reading comics. Walt Disney characters are the favorites, but Garfield, Charlie Brown, and Asterix are also very popular.

Computer games are also popular.

19

History of Italy

Rome was founded in 753 B.C. The Romans went on to conquer most of Europe, and Italy became the center of their vast empire.

In the fifth century A.D., barbarians such as the Huns, Goths, and Vandals from Northern Europe invaded Italy, and the Roman Empire fell.

For many centuries after the fall of the Roman Empire, Italy was divided into small states. The French, Spanish, Arabs, and Austrians all tried to conquer Italy for themselves.

In the nineteenth century, the people rebelled against foreign occupation. The people's hero, Giuseppe Garibaldi, successfully led the fight in 1860.

In 1870, Italy was united into one independent country, with Rome as its capital. Victor Emmanuel II was proclaimed King of Italy.

During World War I, Italy fought on the side of Britain and France. After the war, Benito Mussolini became dictator in 1922. Under his rule, in 1940, Italy entered World War II on the side of Germany.

1922

After World War II, Italy became a republic. In 1958 Italy joined France, West Germany, Belgium, Luxembourg, and the Netherlands to form the European Economic Community.

1958

Famous Italians

Marco Polo (1254–1324) Explorer who traveled from Europe to Asia.

Christopher Columbus (1451–1506) Explorer who reached the West Indies and America.

Leonardo da Vinci (1452–1519) Artist who painted the most famous painting in the world, the Mona Lisa, now in the Louvre in Paris.

Michelangelo Buonarroti (1475–1564) Artist who sculpted the famous statue of David, now in Florence.

Antonio Vivaldi (1678–1741) Musician whose famous work includes The Four Seasons.

Galileo Galilei (1564–1642) Scientist who invented the astronomical telescope.

Famous places

Every year, millions of tourists come to Italy from all over the world. The country has many art treasures and historic remains as well as beautiful countryside. These are some of the places they come to see.

Courmayeur is a famous ski resort near Mont Blanc. It has a French name because it is so close to the French border.

il canale
canal

Venice is a unique city, built on hundreds of tiny islands, with canals for streets and **gondolas** for buses. St. Mark's Square is the largest and most famous in Venice.

The **Ponte Vecchio** (Old Bridge) crosses the river Arno in Florence. It is lined with workshops and houses.

Florence is a beautiful city, full of masterpieces of painting and sculpture, as well as famous buildings.

Capri is a small island off the coast of Naples where the Roman emperor Tiberius built several villas. Tourists like to admire the views and, of course, sunbathe and swim.

Pompeii was an ancient Roman town near Naples. It was buried by lava and ash from Mount Vesuvius in A.D. 79. Today you can visit the ruins, and see houses, streets, shops, and even Latin graffiti on the walls.

la torre
tower

Parts of the rocky coast of Sicily are covered in orange trees and plants called oleanders. Visitors can also see remains of ancient Greek buildings.

The Leaning Tower of Pisa is one of the most famous sights in Italy. The tower leans so much that tourists are no longer allowed to climb up the spiral staircase inside.

There are boat trips around Lake Maggiore. The palace on the tiny island of Isola Bella was built for Isabella, the wife of Count Carlo Borromeo.

l'isola
island

Festivals

Italians love celebrations. There are many festivals during the year. Some take place all over Italy, and some are held just in certain regions. Many villages have their own special feast days.

The week before Ash Wednesday is Carnival time. All over Italy people wear costumes, and there are lots of fairs and parades with floats. The Carnival in Venice is spectacular, with gorgeous costumes and processions of gondolas.

il carnevale
carnival

la gara
race

il cavallo
horse

On July 2 and on August 15, a horse race called the **Palio** is run in Siena. People from the different quarters of the town dress up in medieval costumes, and there are processions to the main square. Here, riders from each quarter compete in the race. The prize is an embroidered banner.

In summer, in towns and villages all over Italy, people have fairs sponsored by different political parties.

There are picnics and barbecues, food stalls, open-air discos, bands, singers, and pop concerts.

Most towns and villages celebrate the feast of their patron saint with a procession. A statue of the saint is carried through the streets and people follow with candles and flowers.

la statua
statue

In the wine-producing areas, people celebrate the end of the grape harvest in the autumn. They hold fairs and dances, and taste the new wine. Often special foods from the region are sold in the markets.

On December 7, in Milan, the feast of the city's patron saint, St. Ambrose, is celebrated with a market fair around his church. There are stalls selling doughnuts, cotton candy, and special sausages, as well as gifts.

On January 6, **La Befana** (an old ragged woman who rides a broomstick) brings sweets to children in Rome. But if they have been naughty, she leaves them a piece of coal instead.

i fuochi d'artificio
fireworks

At the New Year, people in Naples set off fireworks and throw old dishes out of the windows, to show they are making a new start. All the ships in the harbor toot, and there are huge firework displays.

25

Speaking Italian

You will find some useful Italian words on the following pages, plus some simple phrases to help you to ask for things.

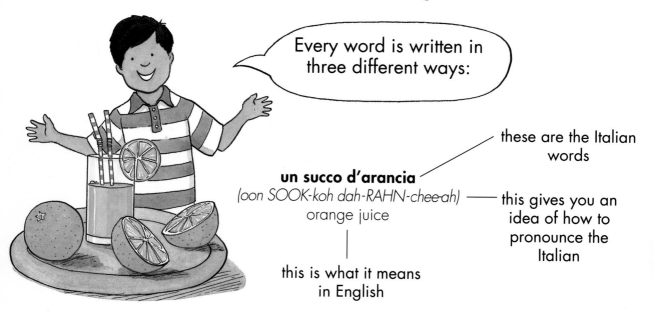

Every word is written in three different ways:

these are the Italian words

un succo d'arancia
(oon SOOK-koh dah-RAHN-chee-ah)
orange juice

this gives you an idea of how to pronounce the Italian

this is what it means in English

In each speech bubble you will find an Italian phrase, a guide to pronouncing it, and its English meaning. In the back of the book, you will find a Guide that will help you make the different Italian sounds. The best way to practice is by saying the words aloud—if possible, to someone who knows how to pronounce them correctly.

the Italian words

how to pronounce the Italian words

the English translation

Vorrei un gelato
(vohr-REH-ee oon jeh-LAH-toh)
I would like ice cream

Making friends

Here are some simple Italian phrases to use when you want to make friends.

Sì
(SEE)
Yes

Ciao. Come ti chiami?
(chee-AH-oh. KOH-meh tee key-AH-mee?)
Hello. What is your name?

Mi chiamo Maria. E tu?
(mee kee-AH-moh Mah-REE-ah. Eh tOO?)
My name is Maria. and yours?

No
(noh)
No

Per favore
(pehr fah-VOH-reh)
Please

Grazie
(GRAH-tsee-eh)
Thank you

Ciao
(chee-AH-oh)
Hello

Dove stai?
(DOH-veh STAH-ee?)
Where are you staying?

Sto laggiù.
(STOH lah-JOO)
I'm staying over there.

Arrivederci
(ahr-ree-veh-DAIR-chee)
Good-bye

Buongiorno
(boo-OWN jee-OHR-noh)
Good morning

Buona sera
(boo-OH-nah SAY-rah)
Good evening

Scusami
(SKOO-zah-mee)
Excuse me

Mi dispiace
(mee dee-spee-AH-cheh)
I'm sorry

Quanti anni hai?
(koo-AHN-tee AHN-nee AH-ee?)
How old are you?

Ho sette anni.
(OH SEHT-teh AHN-nee)
I am seven.

Signore
(seen-YOH-reh)
Mr., Sir

Signora
(seen-YOH-rah)
Mrs., Madam

Parli inglese?
(PAHR-lee een-GLAY-zeh?)
Do you speak English?

Signorina
(seen-yoh-REE-nah)
Miss

27

un'insalata mista
(oon een-sah-LAH-tah MEES-tah)
mixed salad

una pizza
(oo-nah PEET-sah)
pizza

il menù
(eel meh-NOO)
menu

un bicchiere
(oon bee-kee-EH-reh)
glass

un pasticcino
(oon pahs-tee-CHEE-noh)
cupcake

il cameriere
(eel cah-meh-ree-AIR-reh)
waiter

Here are some people ordering food and drink at a café. They are using the word **Vorrei**, which means **I would like**. Using this word you can order any of the items around the picture.

Che cosa desiderano?
(KAY COH-zah deh-ZEE-dair-ah-noh?)
What would you like?

Vorrei un panino con prosciutto e uno Coca-Cola.
(vohr-REH-ee oon pah-NEE-noh kohn proh-SHOOT-toh eh OO-na Coca-Cola.)
I would like a ham sandwich and a Coca-Cola.

un gelato alla fragola
(oon jeh-LAH-toh AHL-lah FRAH-goh-lah)
strawberry ice cream

una bottiglia d'acqua
(OO-nah boht-TEEL-yah DAH-koo-ah)
bottled water

una brioche
*(OO-nah
bree-OHSH)*
sweet roll

un panino con salame
*(oon pahn-NEE-noh
kohn sah-LAH-meh)*
salami on a roll

la pasta
(lah PAHS-tah)
pasta

il conto
(eel KOHN-toh)
bill

l'olio e l'aceto
*(LOH-lee-oh
eh lah-CHAY-toh)*
oil and vinegar

> **Quale gusto—fragola,
> cioccolato o crema?**
> *(koo-AH-leh GOOS-toh—FRAH-goh-lah,
> choh-koh-LAH-toh oh KREH-mah?)*
> Which flavor—strawberry,
> chocolate, or vanilla?

> **Vorrei un gelato.**
> *(vohr-REH-ee oon jeh-LAH-toh)*
> I would like ice cream.

> **Cameriere! Il conto, per
> favore.**
> *(kah-meh-ree-AIR-reh! eel KOHN-toh,
> pehr fah-VOH-reh)*
> Waiter! The bill please.

la cameriera
*(lah cah-meh-
ree-AIR-rah)*
waitress

il sale e il pepe
*(eel SAH-leh eh eel
PEH-peh)*
salt and pepper

delle patate fritte
*(DEHL-leh pah-TAH-teh
FREET-teh)*
French fries

29

la marmellata
(lah mahr-mehl-LAH-tah)
jam

le caramelle
(leh kah-rah-MEHL-leh)
candy

le olive
(leh oh-LEE-veh)
olives

le uova
(leh woo-OH-vah)
eggs

il latte
(eel LAHt-teh)
milk

il pane
(eel PAH-neh)
bread

le pesche
(leh PES-keh)
peaches

i biscotti
(ee bee-SKOHT-tee)
biscuits

The children are shopping for fruit **(frutta)** and vegetables **(verdura)** in a grocery store **(fruttivendolo-alimentari)**.

Desidera?
(deh-ZEE-deh-rah?)
What would you like?

Vorrei un chilo di mele per favore.
(vohr-REH-ee oon KEE-loh dee MEH-leh pehr fah-VOHR-reh)
I would like one kilo (2 lbs) of apples please.

il pollo
(eel POHL-loh)
chicken

il giornale
(eel jee-or-NAH-leh)
newspaper

la torta
*(lah
TOHR-tah)*
cake

le zucchine
*(leh
dzoo-KEE-neh)*
zucchini

il salame
*(eel
sah-LAH-meh)*
salami

il fumetto
(eel foo-MEHT-toh)
comics

Around the pictures are some useful words for things you might want to buy in other shops using the same word **Vorrei.**

le melanzane
(leh meh-lahn-TSAH-neh)
eggplant

Quante ne vuole?
(koo-AHN-teh neh voo-OH-leh?)
How many would you like?

il formaggio
(eel foo-MAH-joh)
cheese

Due lattughe per favore.
*(Doo-eh laht-TOO-gay,
pehr fah-VOH-reh)*
Two heads of lettuce, please.

i francobolli
(ee frahn-koh-BOHL-lee)
stamps

il pesce
(eel PEH-sheh)
fish

i pomodori
*(ee
poh-moh-DOH-ree)*
tomatoes

la crema per il sole
*(lah CREH-mah
pehr eel SOH-leh)*
suntan lotion

Index

due (DOO-eh) two — 2
uno (OO-nah) one — 1
quattro (koo-AHT-troh) four — 4
tre (TREH) three — 3
sei (SAY) six — 6
cinque (CHEEN-koo-eh) five — 5
otto (OHT-toh) eight — 8
sette (SEHT-teh) seven — 7
dieci (dee-EH-chee) ten — 10
nove (NOH-veh) nine — 9
gennaio (jen-EYE-oh) January

nero (NEH-roh) black

bianco (bee-AHN-koh) white

rosso (ROHS-hoh) red

arancio (ah-RAHN-chee-oh) orange

verde (VEHR-deh) green

blu (BLOO) blue

lunedì (loo-neh-DEE) Monday

martedì (mahr-teh-DEE) Tuesday

mercoledì (mehr-koh-leh-DEE) Wednesday

giovedì (joh-veh-DEE) Thursday

venerdì (veh-nair-DEE) Friday

sabato (SAH-bah-toh) Saturday

domenica (doh-MEH-nee-kah) Sunday

dicembre (dee-CHEHM-breh) December

febbraio (feb-BREYE-oh) February

marzo (MAHRT-soh) March

aprile (ah-PREE-leh) April

maggio (MAHJ-joh) May

guigno (JOON-yoh) June

luglio (LOOL-yoh) July

agosto (ah-GOHS-stoh) August

settembre (seht-TEHM-breh) September

ottobre (okt-TOH-breh) October

novembre (noh-VEHM-breh) November